Supporting Dyslexic Learners in the Secondary Curriculum

Moira Thomson, MBE

PARTNERSHIPS WITH PARENTS OF SECONDARY SCHOOL STUDENTS WITH DYSLEXIA

First published in Great Britain by Dyslexia Scotland in 2007

Second edition for schools in England published in 2017 by CPD Bytes Ltd

ISBN 978-1-912146-29-1

This booklet is 1.5 in the series

Supporting Dyslexic Learners in the Secondary Curriculum (England)

Supporting Dyslexic Learners in the Secondary Curriculum   Moira Thomson, MBE

Complete set comprises 25 booklets

1.0   Dyslexia: Secondary Teachers' Guides

1.1   Identification and Assessment of Dyslexia at Secondary School
1.2   Dyslexia: Underpinning Skills for the Secondary Curriculum
1.3   Dyslexia: Reasonable Adjustments to Classroom Management
1.4   Dyslexia: Role of the Secondary School SENCo (Dyslexia Specialist Teacher)
1.5   Partnerships with Parents of Secondary School Students with Dyslexia
1.6   Dyslexia: ICT Support in the Secondary Curriculum
1.7   Dyslexia and Examinations (Reasonable Adjustments & Access Arrangements)
1.8   Dyslexia: Information for Guidance, Pastoral & Behaviour Support Teachers (2013)
1.9   Dyslexia: Learning Styles and Study Skills for the Secondary Curriculum NEW
1.10   Dyslexia: Role of the Teaching Assistant NEW
1.11   Dyslexia: Co-occurring & Overlapping Issues (Specific Learning Difficulties) NEW

2.0   Dyslexia: Subject Teachers' Guides
2.1   Dyslexia: Art & Design Subjects
2.2   Dyslexia: Drama (Performing Arts; Theatre Studies)
2.3   Dyslexia: English (Communication)
2.4   Dyslexia: Home Economics (Child Development; Food & Nutrition)
2.5   Dyslexia: ICT Subjects (Business Subjects; Computer Science)
2.6   Dyslexia: Mathematics (Statistics)
2.7   Dyslexia: Modern Foreign Languages
2.8   Dyslexia: Music
2.9   Dyslexia: Physical Education (Sports; Games; Dance)
2.10   Dyslexia: Science Subjects (Biology; Chemistry; General Science; Physics)
2.11   Dyslexia: Social Subjects (Economics; Geography; History; Citizenship Studies; Philosophy; Religious Studies)
2.12   Dyslexia: The Classics (Classical Greek; Latin; Classical Civilisations) (2013)
2.13   Dyslexia: Media Studies NEW
2.14   Dyslexia: Social Sciences (Anthropology; Archaeology; Humanities; Psychology; Sociology) NEW

Foreword by Dr Gavin Reid, formerly senior lecturer in the Department of Educational Studies, Moray House School of Education, University of Edinburgh. An experienced teacher, educational psychologist, university lecturer, researcher and author, he has made over 1000 conference and seminar presentations in more than 40 countries and has authored, co-authored and edited many books for teachers and parents.

ACKNOWLEDGEMENTS

Moira Thomson would like to thank the following for making possible the original publication of this important series of booklets:

- ✦ Dyslexia Scotland for supporting the publication and distribution of the original editions of these booklets
- ✦ The Royal Bank of Scotland for an education grant that funded Dyslexia Scotland's support
- ✦ Dr Gavin Reid for his encouragement over the years – and for writing the Foreword to these booklets
- ✦ Dr Jennie Guise of DysGuise Ltd for her support and professional advice
- ✦ The committee of Dyslexia Scotland South East for their support
- ✦ Alasdair Andrew for all his hard work and unfailing confidence
- ✦ Colleagues Maggie MacLardie and Janet Hodgson for helpful comments
- ✦ Cameron Halfpenny for proof reading and editing these booklets
- ✦ Current and former students, whose achievements make it all worthwhile

Moira Thomson MBE

2017

FOREWORD by Dr Gavin Reid

The Dyslexia booklets written by Moira Thomson have been widely circulated and highly appreciated by teachers throughout Scotland and beyond. I know they have also been used by teachers in a number of countries and this is testimony to the skills of Moira in putting together these booklets in the different subject areas of the secondary school curriculum.

It is therefore an additional privilege for me to be approached again by Moira to update this Foreword to the compendium of books developed by Moira in association with Dyslexia Scotland.

These updated guides are for all teachers - they contain information that will be directly relevant and directly impact on the practice of every teacher in every secondary school in the country. It is heartening to note that the guides again provide a very positive message to readers. The term Dyslexia is not exclusive to the challenges experienced by learners with dyslexia, but there is now a major thrust towards focussing on the strengths and particularly what they **can** do - and not what they 'can't do'. It is important to obtain a learning profile which can be shared with the student.

Moira encapsulates these points in these updated booklets. The focus is on supporting learners and helping them overcome the barriers to learning. At the same time it is important that learners with dyslexia, particularly in the secondary school develop responsibility for their own learning. The acquisition of self-sufficiency in learning and self-knowledge is an important aspect of acquiring efficient learning skills for students with dyslexia. It is this that will stand them in good stead as they approach important examinations and the transition to tertiary education and the workplace. For that reason these guides are extremely important and need to be available to all teachers. Moira ought to be congratulated in endeavouring to achieve this.

The breadth of coverage in these guides is colossal. Moira Thomson has met this immense task with professionalism and clarity of expression and the comprehensiveness of the guides in covering the breadth of the curriculum is commendable.

As well as including all secondary school subjects the guides also provide information on the crucial aspects of supporting students preparing for examinations, the use of information and communication technology, information for parents, details of the assessment process and the skills that underpin learning. It is important to consider the view that learners with dyslexia are first and foremost 'learners' and therefore it is important that their learning skills are developed fully. It is too easy to place the emphasis on developing literacy skills at the expense of other important aspects of learning. The guides will reinforce this crucial point that the learning skills of all students with dyslexia can be developed to a high level.

The guides do more than provide information on dyslexia; they are a staff development resource and one that can enlighten and educate all teachers in secondary schools. I feel certain they will continue to be warmly appreciated. The guides have already been widely appreciated by teachers and school management as well as parents and other professionals, but the real winners have been and will continue to be the **students** with dyslexia. It is they who will ultimately benefit and the guides will help them fulfil their potential and make learning a positive and successful school experience.

Dr Gavin Reid
April 2016

WHAT IS DYSLEXIA?

Dyslexia is widely recognised as a specific difficulty in learning to read.

Research shows that dyslexia may affect more than the ability to read, write and spell – and there is a growing body of research on these 'co-occurring' factors.

The Rose Report[1] identifies dyslexia as *'a developmental difficulty of language learning and cognition that primarily affects the skills involved in accurate and fluent word reading and spelling, characterised by difficulties in phonological awareness, verbal memory and verbal processing speed.'*

Dyslexia is a learning difficulty that primarily affects the skills involved in accurate and fluent word reading and spelling.

Characteristic features of dyslexia are difficulties in phonological awareness, verbal memory and verbal processing speed.

Dyslexia occurs across the range of intellectual abilities.

It is best thought of as a continuum, not a distinct category, and there are no clear cut-off points.

Co-occurring difficulties may be seen in aspects of language, motor co-ordination, mental calculation, concentration and personal organisation, but these are not, <u>by themselves,</u> markers of dyslexia.

A good indication of the severity and persistence of dyslexic difficulties can be gained by examining how the individual responds or has responded to well-founded intervention.

Rose Report page 10

Dyslexia *exists in all cultures and across the range of abilities and socio-economic backgrounds. It is a hereditary, life-long, neuro-developmental condition. Unidentified, dyslexia is likely to result in low self-esteem, high stress, atypical behaviour, and low achievement.*[2]

Estimates of the prevalence of dyslexia vary according to the definition adopted but research suggests that dyslexia may significantly affect the literacy attainment of between 4% and 10% of children.

---

[1] Rose, J (2009*) Identifying and Teaching Children and Young People with Dyslexia and Literacy Difficulties* DCFS Publications - independent report to the Secretary of State for Children, Schools & Families June 2009
http://webarchive.nationalarchives.gov.uk/20130401151715/http://www.education.gov.uk/publications/eOr deringDownload/00659-2009DOM-EN.pdf

[2] From Scottish Government working definition of dyslexia
http://www.gov.scot/Topics/Education/Schools/welfare/ASL/dyslexia

TEACHERS' RESPONSIBILITIES RE LEARNERS WITH DYSLEXIA

References: Part 6 of the Equality Act 2010; Part 3 of the Children and Families Act 2014

All children/young people are entitled to an education appropriate to their needs that promotes high standards and the fulfilment of potential - to enable them to:

- achieve their best
- become confident individuals living fulfilling lives
- make a successful transition into adulthood, whether into employment, further or higher education or training

SEND Code of Practice 0-25[3]

All schools have duties towards individual young people to identify and address any Special Educational Needs/Disability (SEND). Dyslexia that has a substantial, long-term, adverse impact on day-to-day learning may be identified as both SEN and a disability.

Teachers' responsibilities for meeting the needs of dyslexic learners are the same as those for all students, and should include approaches that avoid unnecessary dependence on written text.

Teachers have a responsibility to provide a suitably differentiated subject curriculum, accessible to all learners, that provides each with the opportunity to develop and apply individual strengths – and to ensure that learners with SEND get the support they need to access this. Rose[4] suggests that all teachers should have 'core knowledge' of dyslexia characteristics – to help them to make adjustments to their practice that will prevent discrimination and substantial disadvantage.

Dyslexia may be difficult for some teachers to identify in a subject context – some think that dyslexia has little or no impact in their subject – others believe that dyslexia will have been resolved at primary school. The impact of unsupported dyslexia on learning in secondary subject classrooms may be profound, and result in a mismatch between a student's apparent subject ability and the quality (and quantity) of written work.

While subject teachers are not expected to diagnose dyslexia without specialist input, they should be aware of its core characteristics and likely manifestations in the classroom so they may refer students to the SENCo (or specialist teacher) for assessment. Many schools have checklists and questionnaires in place to help teachers identify possible SEN and subject teachers should use these and follow established procedures when they suspect that dyslexia might be present.[5]

---

[3] SEND Code of Practice 0-25
https://www.gov.uk/government/uploads/system/uploads/attachment_data/file/398815/SEND_Code_of_Practice_January_2015.pdf
[4] Rose Report (2009) page 17
[5] A version of a Dyslexia Indicators Checklist for secondary age students is provided at the end of this booklet

THE SEND CODE OF PRACTICE 0-25
Engaging with parents

...it is in the child's best interests for a positive dialogue between parents, teachers and others to be maintained...

The SEND Code of Practice 0-25 provides statutory guidance for organisations that work with and support children and young people with SEND - and sets out duties, policies and procedures relating to Part 3 of the 2014 Act that apply to England. The duties placed on all educational establishments include clearly defined rights and responsibilities of parents.

Local authorities must ensure that parents and children/young people are provided with the information, advice and support necessary to enable them to participate in discussions and decisions about their support. Every local authority now has to publish a Local Offer - and each school must identify provision that feeds into this – in order to give parents a clear understanding of what support individual schools are able to provide for students.

The SEND Code of Practice 0-25 requires schools to share information by:
- providing information to feed into the Local Offer being co-ordinated by the local authority
- publishing a SEN Report on what they offer children/young people with SEND which identifies approaches to supporting individual students
- collaborating and communicating with both students and parents when drawing up policies and procedures
- reporting to parents on school SEN policy – and its implementation
- notifying parents and students of any decisions being made about their individual support and providing annual progress reports to parents

SEN SUPPORT
While parents have welcomed the greater focus on personal goals and improved rights and protections for young people, some are concerned that dyslexic students may lose out on support in school. But **the definition of special educational needs has not been changed.** The former school action and school action plus categories of SEN have been replaced with a single category of SEN Support - a graduated approach to supporting students identified as having SEND – which allows greater flexibility in provision to support the needs of individual dyslexic students.

The Department for Education has published a SEND Guide for parents/carers.[6] This guide is intended to provide some information covering the whole system and **Parent Carer Forums**[7] (representative local groups of parents and carers of children/young people with disabilities) have been established in most areas - local authorities and schools are actively encouraged to work with them.

---

[6] https://www.gov.uk/government/publications/send-guide-for-parents-and-carers
[7] http://www.nnpcf.org.uk/

THE GRADUATED APPROACH TO SEND
Assess – Plan – Do – Review – a role for parents

More than 1.5 million children and young people in England have been identified as having special educational needs or disabilities (SEND) – so it is clear that most teachers will teach at least one pupil with SEND in every class. Dyslexics are the largest single group of students with SEND in secondary schools - and 10-15% of all students who have SEND will also have dyslexia – one reason why the Dyslexia Friendly Schools initiative began.

The first step in responding to secondary students who may have dyslexia is the provision of high quality subject teaching, differentiated to meet the needs of all students - with reasonable adjustments made to remove barriers to learning – e.g. copies of class notes are distributed to all students to remove any disadvantage to those with dyslexia.

The responsibility and accountability for progress of students who have dyslexia lies with the subject teacher – though the SENCo and the school's Learning Support team may be involved in tailoring interventions that are additional to or different from what is provided for all students – in order to meet individual needs.

SEND provision for dyslexia should be needs-led and take the form of a four-part cycle of: **assess-plan-do-review**. This is known as "the graduated approach".

When a subject teacher becomes aware of barriers to and 'gaps' in a student's learning - they should **ASSESS** the reasons why the student is not making the expected progress so that effective SEN support may be put in place. **Parents are informed of concerns** and invited to contribute their views and experience to the assessment process. When a student is already known to be dyslexic, this stage will focus on how the dyslexia affects learning in the subject curriculum and barriers to learning met by individuals.

Schools have their own policies and procedures for involving parents in the assessment of students' additional learning needs – and these often include questionnaires or completing checklists of their concerns (see example at the end of this booklet) to help clarify any underlying issues that contribute to a student experiencing difficulties. Information provided by parents may help the SENCo determine the focus of any further assessment – e.g. screening for dyslexia.

Once the reasons for a student's lack of progress in a subject have been identified, the subject teacher may then **PLAN** provision to meet the needs identified – taking account of:
- the information obtained from individual assessments
- the views of the parents (and the student)
- changes/adjustments to day-to-day subject teaching required

All teachers and support staff should be made aware of individual students' needs, the support provided and any teaching strategies or approaches required.

SEND Code of Practice 0-25

This is difficult in secondary schools where many different teaching and support staff are involved with each student. Some schools have adopted a student profile (see example at the end of this booklet) or 'passport' to help disseminate important information. This will provide essential data about the student's individual needs, suggestions for meeting these needs in different subject classrooms and details of any targeted interventions in place.

SEN support plans (or Individual Education Plans) are based on individual student needs and are subject-specific - identifying learning outcomes in a subject and the support to be provided to help the student achieve these. Dyslexic students and their parents attend meetings to plan and review SEN Support Plans. The timescale for the review of progress and evaluation of the effectiveness of the support provided is set at this meeting.

The implementation of the SEN support plan is the - **DO** – part of the graduated approach – and is closely followed by **REVIEW**. The teacher makes the agreed adjustments in the classroom and monitors how effective these are in helping the students achieve the specified outcomes in the plan – e.g. pairing a dyslexic student with a 'reading buddy' to help keep up with class activities in Geography. If the student keeps up, the planned intervention is effective and should be kept in place. Any adjustments to planned support should be made immediately without waiting for the set review date – e.g. an appropriate substitute must be nominated and trained to take over if a 'reading buddy' is absent.

Parents - and students – will attend a formal REVIEW of progress towards achieving the specified outcomes in the SEN support plan around the date set. This does not have to be a full, formal meeting – especially if planned support is having the desired effect – but it is important that their views are heard – and taken into account when planning support for any new outcomes set.

The graduated approach starts again as REVIEW flows into ASSESS (progress) and PLAN (new outcomes). This is sometimes referred to as a graduated 'spiral' which aims to resolve barriers to learning and lead to academic success.

PARENT-TEACHER PARTNERSHIPS

All parents/carers have concerns about their children's progress and wish to play active parts in their education. Some parents/carers of dyslexic children will need a high level of support from the school to help them understand the challenges their children may face in the secondary curriculum and to explain any additional support that may be provided.

All school/home communications should be clear, positive and constructive in order to develop a shared understanding that everyone has the student's best interests at heart.

In order to help parents/carers begin to accept that dyslexia will be a key aspect of their children's learning for the whole of their time at school, teachers should make efforts to:

- Engage in an on-going dialogue with parents/carers that is sympathetic and non-judgmental, with all teachers listening to all parental concerns
- Demonstrate that the school has a dyslexia friendly ethos, providing a structure for appropriate assessment of dyslexia, linked to the demands of the secondary subject curriculum
- Ensure that dyslexic students have access to a subject curriculum and materials at an appropriate level, in an appropriate format
- Offer a well-planned programme of additional support based on appropriate individual assessments and the demands of the subject curriculum
- Anticipate difficulties and stress arising from the impact of dyslexia on organisational and short-term memory by working together with parents/carers and students themselves to develop strategies to deal with problems concerning:
    - copying down homework at the end of the lesson
    - sending home notes and newsletters
    - relaying verbal messages
    - the amount or type of homework
- Develop a shared understanding that there is no 'quick fix' or 'cure' for dyslexia and that supporting the progress of dyslexic students may be a long uphill struggle for subject teachers
- Offer support for a student's social and emotional needs as they arise

There are additional issues that parents/carers of dyslexic students may face from time to time that might be eased only by contact with others whose children also struggle with dyslexia. These include:

- **Confusion** about what dyslexia is and how it was identified/assessed
- **Guilt** about the possible inherited/genetic nature of dyslexia
- **Concern** about what the future may hold for their children
- **Anger** – often irrational - at the school, the child, self and partner for a number of reasons, some apparently unconnected with dyslexia

- **Frustration** at feelings of helplessness, sometimes linked to limitations set by their own dyslexia
- **Anxiety** about their children's feelings of confusion, distress, anger and frustration – the '*why me?*' question
- **Over-protectiveness** developed by living with a dyslexic child and watching the daily struggle just to be 'normal'
- **Stress** because the whole family can be affected by something as simple as inappropriate homework
- **Exasperation** because it is sometimes hard to convince education professionals that parents/carers really do know their children best
- **Despair** caused by some or all of the above

In order the help them get through these feelings, the school should make parents/carers of dyslexic students aware of outside agencies and support groups such as the local branch of the British Dyslexia Association – or perhaps the SENCo or SEND Governor might form a group within the school where they may share experiences and support each other.

When parents are contacted about their child's dyslexia – whether raising the possibility for the first time or arranging for a progress review, it would be useful for the SENCo to send home some general information about dyslexia as well as any checklist or questionnaire for them to complete as part of the assessment/review process.

SUBJECT TEACHERS' GRADUATED APPROACH TO DYSLEXIA SUPPORT SHOULD INCLUDE:

- Awareness of the need to involve parents in supporting their dyslexic children

- Sensitivity to the learning differences related to dyslexia that may cause difficulties within the subject curriculum

- Acknowledgement of the very severe difficulties some dyslexic learners experience due to failure to master early stages of literacy and numeracy

- Understanding that dyslexia is developmental in nature and that some students who coped with the early stages of literacy acquisition may begin to experience difficulties with higher order skills and processing issues in the secondary curriculum

- Selection or design of appropriate teaching and learning programmes that match the range of all abilities, within the curricular framework of the school

- Commitment to the need to reduce barriers to learning linked to the delivery of the curriculum as well as those due to the impact of dyslexia

- Acceptance that some dyslexic students may require additional support and to consult parents, colleagues and the student to determine how to provide this

- Willingness to ask for advice and support from the SENCo and/or specialist teacher if a dyslexic learner does not make the expected progress towards achieving curricular outcomes and consider whether there is a need for a SEN Support Plan

- Understanding that, while dyslexia is not linked to ability, able dyslexic learners may persistently underachieve

- Knowledge that many dyslexic learners use strategies such as misbehaviour or illness for coping with difficulties they do not necessarily understand themselves

- Taking account of the difficulties experienced by dyslexic learners when reviewing progress so that subject knowledge and ability are assessed fairly by making reasonable adjustments for exams (Access Arrangements) that reflect the additional support usually provided in the classroom

Dyslexic learners constantly meet barriers to learning across the curriculum and may become discouraged very quickly due to lack of initial success in subject classes. This may result in subject teachers assuming that they are inattentive or lazy, when they are actually working much harder than their classmates, but with little apparent effect.

FURTHER READING

Hornigold, J (2013) *Help! My Child Has Dyslexia: A Practical Guide for Parents* Cheshire, LDA

Hultquist, AM (2013) *Can I Tell You About Dyslexia? A Guide for Friends, Family and Professionals* London, Jessica Kingsley Publishers

Likierman, H & Muter, V (2008) *Dyslexia: A parents' guide to dyslexia, dyspraxia and other learning difficulties* London, Vermillion (Random House)
This book starts by correcting common misconceptions of learning difficulties in the press and popular literature, and addresses the conflicting approaches and advice from 'experts'.

NASEN (2015) *Working in Partnership with Parents and Carers*
http://www.nasen.org.uk/resources/resources.working-in-partnership-with-parents-and-carers.html

Ostler, C (1999) *Dyslexia - A Parent's Survival Guide* Surrey, Ammonite Books
A down-to-earth 'survival' guide, which gives advice and suggestions for parents who find bringing up a dyslexic child both frustrating and worrying - strategies are suggested for coping in a positive way with the problems of the dyslexic at home and at school.

Parent Champions (2013) *Understanding Dyslexia – A Guide for Parents, Carers and Young People*
http://www.parentchampions.org.uk/wp-content/uploads/2013/02/parentDyslexiaSecondaryBook-v2.pdf

Reid, G (2011) *DYSLEXIA: A Complete Guide for Parents* (2nd Edition) London, John Wiley & Sons
This book provides the unique insights of a noted educational psychologist on what sort of supportive role parents can play in the life of their dyslexic child.

Reid, G & Green, S (2007) *100 Ideas for Supporting Students with Dyslexia* London, Continuum

Riddick B, Wolfe J, Lumsden D, *(2004) Dyslexia: A Practical Guide for Teachers and Parents (Resource Materials for Teachers)* Abingdon, Routledge
This book focuses on realistic strategies for non-specialists to use when working with pupils who have dyslexia.

Thomson, M (2007) *Supporting Students with Dyslexia at Secondary School – every class teacher's guide to removing barriers and raising attainment* London, Routledge Ch. 10

DYSLEXIA INDICATORS AT THE SECONDARY STAGE (PHOTOCOPIABLE)

Dyslexia is more than an isolated defect in reading or spelling. The problem may be perceptual, auditory receptive, memory-based or a processing deficit.

Subject teachers are not expected to be able to diagnose these difficulties as such, but some general indications are listed below. If several of these are observed frequently in the classroom, subject teachers should tick the relevant boxes to identify issues when referring a student for further investigation.

Student Name: _____ Class: _____ Date: _____

- ❏ Quality of written work does not adequately reflect the known ability of the student in the subject

- ❏ Good orally but very little written work is produced – many incomplete assignments

- ❏ Disappointing performance in timed tests and other assessments

- ❏ Poor presentation of work – e.g. illegibility, mixed upper and lower case, unequal spacing, copying errors, misaligned columns (especially in Maths)

- ❏ Poor organisational skills – the student is unable to organise self or work efficiently; carries either all books or wrong ones; frequently forgets to hand in work

- ❏ Sequencing poor – student appears to jump from one theme to another, apparently for no reason

- ❏ Inability to memorise (especially in Maths and Modern Languages) even after repeated practice

- ❏ Inability to hold numbers in short-term memory while performing calculations

- ❏ Symbol and shape confusion (especially in Maths)

- ❏ Complains of headaches when reading; sometimes sees patterns/distortions in printed text; says that words move around the page or that text is glaring at them

- ❏ Unable to carry out operations one day which were previously done adequately

- ❏ Unable to take in and carry out more than one instruction at a time

- ❏ Poor depth perception – e.g. clumsy and uncoordinated, bumps into things, difficulty judging distance, catching balls, etc.

- ❏ Poor self-image – lacking in confidence, fear of new situations – may erase large quantities of written work, which is acceptable to the teacher

- ❏ Tires quickly and work seems to be a disproportionate return for the effort involved in producing it

- ❏ Easily distracted – either hyperactive or daydreaming

- ❏ **Other – details below**

```
┌─────────────────────────────────────────────────────────────┐
│                                                               │
│                                                               │
│                                                               │
│                                                               │
│                                                               │
│                                                               │
│                                                               │
│                                                               │
└─────────────────────────────────────────────────────────────┘
```

Teacher: _____ Subject: _____

Action/information requested:

- ❏ details of known SEND and support required

- ❏ investigation of SEND and advice on graduated support

- ❏ dyslexia assessment

- ❏ profile of learning needs

- ❏ suggest reasonable adjustments to be made in class

- ❏ suggest learning objectives and outcomes for SEN plan

- ❏ advice re Access arrangements

DYSLEXIA - CONTRIBUTORY FACTORS
Information for parents

Parents may have noticed some of the factors listed below and agree that investigation of dyslexia should be carried out. The SENCo/specialist teacher investigating a student for dyslexia may ask if these factors have been checked; some will be known only to parents, and details may not be required for identification of dyslexia – but parents may find it useful to know of some factors that may have contributed to their child's dyslexia.

1. Birth history - Were there any problems before during or after birth, e.g. a premature birth?

2. Family history - Are others in the family dyslexic? There is usually a genetic factor in developmental dyslexia, though other family members may have varying symptoms and severity.

3. Educational history - Has school experience been difficult? What intervention has there been? How has this helped?

4. General health - Have there been any long illnesses or a physical injury, involving school absence? Could there be any undiagnosed conditions, e.g. mild epilepsy or petit mal, which may look like inattention and cause gaps in learning?

5. Vision - School medicals are not enough. Has vision been checked by an optometrist? Does the child lose the place when reading? Is the student light sensitive or experiences visual stress (print distortions)?

6. Hearing - Has hearing been checked? Did the child have 'glue ear' when younger? This may have hindered auditory perception of sounds in words.

7. Speech and language – Were there delays or deficits in speech and language development (pronunciation of words; vocabulary development; the complexity of spoken language and understanding of language heard)? Was a referral to a speech and language therapist made? Is English the first language in the home? This could have implications for test results, even for visual/spatial aspects of cognitive ability for which oral instructions are given.

8. Co-ordination - Is the student clumsy or accident-prone? Does this affect gross and fine motor movements? Is the student aware of his/her own body in space in relation to people and objects? How is anticipation of the movements of others, e.g. in team games? Dyspraxia might be a possibility if verbal ability is considerably higher than visual-spatial skills in ability tests – so a referral to an occupational therapist might be advisable. Left-handedness is not significantly higher in dyslexics but life is harder for all left-handers. Cross-laterality is not significant either but late development of hand dominance or non-dominance of hand, eye, foot, seems to happen more often in dyslexics.

9. Attention and Emotional Behavioural issues - If these are present, are they primary factors or an outcome of frustration at difficulty in learning? Some behavioural issues appear to be controllable and are intended to disrupt or annoy – but may be rooted in the frustration caused by undiagnosed dyslexia. Other conditions, like Attention Deficit Disorder, with or without Hyperactivity, are involuntary, and disruptive behaviour appears purposeless and puzzling to all concerned. Lack of ability to concentrate is typical of ADD and ADHD, so weaknesses in – e.g. - reading may be a result of this.

10. Communication/relationship issues - This is different from speech and language disorders. Students may have difficulty making eye-contact, communicating and making relationships and showing appropriate behaviour. They may take everything literally – or be unable to 'read' facial expressions or comprehend tone of voice.

11. Self-esteem. Literacy is deemed very important in our culture. It is not surprising that those who find it difficult are very frustrated, depressed and have low self-esteem. People complain about giving labels, but most dyslexics are very pleased to know that there is a reason for their difference.

12. Cognitive abilities - What some people refer to as 'intelligence' is made up of several different cognitive abilities – and dyslexic students often have a 'spiky' or uneven profile of these which is not revealed by an overall standard score. Some may have a high level of verbal comprehension and be able to process language quickly – but be frustrated by their inability to remember simple instructions. Others may have above average non-verbal ability but have difficulty with reading and spelling. Some parents may have been told their child has global learning difficulties – but this does not mean that the child is of low intelligence – there may be an easily explained developmental delay that will respond to specific interventions.

13. Diet supplements and drugs - There is no pill that makes learning to read easy. However, nutritional vulnerability or deficiencies may have an impact on concentration and behaviour so affect learning indirectly - some dyslexics lack a natural production of some essential nutritional ingredients – others may be allergic to food additives.

14. Individual styles for learning - Any assessment of dyslexia will reveal strengths as well as weaknesses. Some dyslexics develop strategies for their own ways of doing things and this should be encouraged.

PARENTAL CONCERNS CHECKLIST (PHOTOCOPIABLE)

Student: _____ Year: _____

Everyone struggles with learning at times – some issues like dyslexia are consistent and persist over time. Are you concerned that your child:

- ❑ Is not learning, communicating or relating to others as well as you expect
- ❑ struggles with reading
- ❑ is losing confidence and motivation – unwilling to go to school

The following list is a general guide to learning issues, not a tool to identify specific learning difficulties - though assessment for dyslexia, dyspraxia or Attention-Deficit Hyperactivity Disorder (ADHD) may be advised for students who display several of these warning signs.

Tick any warning signs that apply to your child - no one knows your child better than you do, so trust your instincts!

For at least the past 6 months, my child has had issues with:

Language

- ❑ understanding instructions or directions
- ❑ repeating what has just been said in proper sequence
- ❑ staying on topic and getting to the point (gets bogged down in details)
- ❑ naming people and objects
- ❑ using appropriate subject vocabulary
- ❑ pronouncing unfamiliar words correctly
- ❑ speaking smoothly, without much halting or use of "filler words" (like "um")
- ❑ understanding humour, puns and idioms

Reading

- ❑ reading age-appropriate content fluently
- ❑ reading aloud or silently with good understanding
- ❑ losing the place often, missing words or lines
- ❑ feeling confident and interested in reading
- ❑ recognising new subject vocabulary quickly
- ❑ accurately decoding unfamiliar words (tends to guess instead)
- ❑ understanding word problems in maths, science etc.

Writing

- ❑ mastering spelling rules
- ❑ spelling the same word consistently and correctly
- ❑ writing legibly at a reasonable speed
- ❑ proofreading and correcting self-generated work
- ❑ expressing ideas in an organized way
- ❑ preparing/organising writing assignments
- ❑ fully developing ideas in writing
- ❑ listening and taking notes at the same time

Social-Emotional

- ❑ participating in a peer group and maintaining positive social status
- ❑ interpreting people's non-verbal cues, "body language," mood and tone of voice
- ❑ frustration and anger/embarrassment – unable to deal with peer pressure,
- ❑ setting realistic social goals
- ❑ maintaining positive self-esteem about learning and getting along with other
- ❑ maintaining confidence about "fitting in" with classmates and other peers

Other

- ❑ learning/remembering new skills
- ❑ remembering facts and numbers
- ❑ lacks a sense of direction/spatial concepts (such as left and right)
- ❑ performs inconsistently on tasks from day to day
- ❑ unable to apply skills from one situation to another
- ❑ struggles to learn new subject skills

If your child displays several of these warning signs, don't hesitate to seek help from the SENCo.

Taking early action can avoid frustration and help prevent your child meeting unexpected barriers to learning in subject classrooms.

EXAMPLE OF STUDENT SEND PROFILE (PHOTOCOPIABLE)

Name: _____ **Form:** _____ **Date:** _____

Teacher: _____ **Subject[8]:** _____

Factors linked to SEND:

Slow and inaccurate reading and problems with sequencing and short-term working memory – consistent with dyslexia (currently being formally assessed)

Impact on the student in the curriculum:

Reading issues

- ☐ slower reading than other students of similar age/ability
- ☐ difficulty decoding unfamiliar words
- ☐ makes errors when reading, especially reading loud
- ☐ difficulty remembering what has just been read
- ☐ cannot always understand on first reading
- ☐ cannot easily locate information in a text
- ☐ loses the place often when reading

Writing issues

- ☐ unable to identify errors in written work e.g. when re-drafting
- ☐ weak spelling - sometimes cannot encode familiar words
- ☐ finds sequencing written work difficult
- ☐ cannot remember instructions
- ☐ difficulty following a sequence of instructions

Number/maths issues

- ☐ cannot hold numbers in short term memory when doing calculations
- ☐ confused about direction – may start calculations in the wrong place
- ☐ cannot process information in graphic/diagrammatic form quickly
- ☐ cannot easily recall learned facts – e.g. tables, formulae, vocabulary
- ☐ unable to show working when doing calculations

Suggested support strategies

- ☐ allow extra time for reading/ allow 'buddy' support to re-read text
- ☐ encourage use of a marker to keep the place
- ☐ give page, paragraph and line numbers & highlight key information in text sources
- ☐ allow the use of a coloured overlay for reading activities
- ☐ allow extra time for extended reading/writing and for all tests
- ☐ issue subject glossary of terminology and meanings
- ☐ allow computer use with spell-check for written work
- ☐ issue copies of class/dictated notes
- ☐ issue formula prompt sheets /vocabulary tapes to aid memory
- ☐ allow calculator/number square use & provide exemplars of Maths problems

---

[8] Subject teachers should retain this summary as a record of a student's usual way of working

HOW PARENTS CAN HELP THEIR DYSLEXIC TEENAGERS (PHOTOCOPIABLE)

Children's first awareness of their dyslexia is often the result of failure at school.

There is a lack of understanding of why they cannot learn like their classmates. They feel that they are to blame for this – they do not know how to get help and they cannot explain the difficulties being experienced. This inevitably leads to low self-esteem.

The longer dyslexia goes unrecognised, the greater the problem becomes. Many boys become frustrated and some develop behavioural difficulties – they may become disruptive and aggressive - even throw their books away because they do not understand why they are still unable to read effectively.

Girls tend to become withdrawn - but often find support with a group of friends – they may and spend time copying work rather than fall behind. As they get older, both boys and girls may become unwilling to go to school, and they may complain of headaches or feeling sick on days when a subject they do not like is on the timetable – or begin selective truancy to avoid subjects where they are struggling. Because of the fragmented nature of the secondary timetable, this truancy may take teachers – and parents - some time to identify.

It is not uncommon for a learner's dyslexia to be hidden by the more obvious behavioural issues displayed in the classroom – and identification of dyslexia may come as a surprise to some secondary teachers. However, many parents have had to deal with the impact of dyslexia at home well before it is recognised by the school – so eventual identification of dyslexia is a huge relief.

Working with the school

If parents become concerned about their child's progress, they should make an appointment to see the form or guidance teacher to discuss their concerns. A student's failure to make progress can result in a very emotional meeting, so parents should prepare in advance of the appointment. A suggested framework might be:

- List the points to be addressed at the meeting.

- Be certain of what you want the outcome of the meeting to be.

- Take someone along to provide moral support – some parents feel intimidated by teachers and some think that teachers may 'talk down' to concerned parents.

- Be positive, firm, calm and confident. This is your child's education and well being – comparisons with other students will not be appropriate.

- Take notes at the meeting – what you are told may be new and confusing, and you may need to refer to it later when a decision has been made.

- Do not agree to anything unless you are absolutely sure. Sometimes you need to reflect on what you have been told, or seek further advice.

- If anything is agreed, set a reasonable time limit for the action to be taken.

- After you have had time to reflect, put in a letter what you understood was discussed and agreed at the meeting and ask the school to confirm that they agree.

- Before leaving the meeting, arrange for a follow up meeting – shortly after the time limit set – with the understanding that the school will contact you immediately if there are any problems.

A firm non-aggressive approach should lead to the development of a good parent/teacher relationship – so be patient and persevering while insisting on an assessment of your child's difficulties.

- insist that information is passed on in good time

- make yourself known to any new teacher and make sure that details of the dyslexia have been passed on

- be diplomatic if a new teacher does not have relevant information – offer to provide details

- try to remain positive despite your own feelings – showing anger and bitterness can have an adverse effect on the child

At home
Homework can be a frustrating and upsetting experience for dyslexics and their parents on a daily basis.

Parents should remember that the purpose of homework is for the student to practise something that is already familiar. If homework is too difficult, they should discuss this with the teacher – and not allow a dyslexic learner to become frustrated because homework tasks are beyond their skills or take too long.

Asking teachers to set smaller amounts of work and/or allow extra time or direct help for completion will often help.

HOMEWORK TIPS FOR PARENTS (PHOTOCOPIABLE)

Homework can be a frustrating and upsetting experience for dyslexic students and their parents on a daily basis. Here are some tips to help make this less traumatic.

First of all, **remember**: the purpose of homework is for the student to practise something that is already familiar. If homework is too difficult, parents should discuss this with the teacher who issued it – and not allow teenagers to become frustrated because homework tasks are beyond their skills or take too long. Asking teachers to set smaller amounts of work and/or allow extra time for completion will often help.

1. Establish a routine

- put a written or visual plan up in a prominent place
- set aside a particular place for homework
- agree a plan as to what happens after arrival home from school - flexible enough to take into account after-school activities

The homework place needs to be quiet with a cleared space for work and equipment at hand e.g. pens, pencils etc. The kitchen table is suitable if close supervision is required.

Parents should work out the best time for homework to be done - keeping in mind that even teenagers may be very tired after school - they have had to work harder than other pupils in class because of their dyslexia – so need a break before doing homework.

2. Getting Started

- break homework tasks into manageable parts
- allow breaks between different tasks
- encourage the production of quality work rather than rushing to finish everything in one sitting – act as a reader/scribe if necessary
- **Do not** arrange for extra homework to help your child catch up - a dyslexic learner can become discouraged when faced with large amounts of extra work

Go over the homework requirements to ensure it is clear what is required – e.g. read instructions aloud to make sure that the task is fully understood. If necessary, help with the first example or two – help with generating ideas for writing tasks and projects before writing starts – e.g. revise subject vocabulary or help to develop a writing plan.

Encourage use of personal strengths to present work – e.g. pictures drawings if the student is an artist. When necessary and appropriate, arrange with the teacher that you will act as a scribe to help get ideas on paper more accurately.

3. Checking and Monitoring Work

Help to check and edit written work. Encourage the use of the computer for written work and research. The use of a spell checker and touch-typing skills will have been taught in school – or Typing Tutor programs may be used at home for additional practice. There are many writing aids for use on the computer – check with the school what software is used, and try to provide this at home too.

If your dyslexic child is slow to complete work - use a timer to find out how much work can be completed in e.g. five minutes – then check with the teacher how long a homework task is expected to take. But remember that if homework is regularly taking too long or is too difficult, you should discuss this with subject staff – and ensure that the need for extra time is recorded as your child's usual way of working to provide evidence for future Access arrangements for exams.

Give lots of praise as homework tasks are completed identifying exactly what they have done well.

4. Organisation
Monitor how much time is spent on homework. Help develop a comprehensive homework plan - including revision as well as set homework tasks. Check that homework as well as the correct books and equipment is taken to school each day.

Provide folders to keep subjects notes and work together - and ensure that they are filed regularly. Colour coding of subjects will help organisation and planning.

If homework is not written down accurately, arrange to check with someone in the same class at the end of the day - or ask teachers to provide written homework instructions or email these for more complex tasks. Liaise with teachers regularly to ensure that all homework tasks and class work is completed correctly and handed in on time.

5. Study Skills
Make sure that your teenager has plans for approaching tasks like essay writing, and study for exams. Help to build up independent work skills and problem-solving strategies – e.g. think about several different ways they could complete a task correctly – and find out who to ask for help if the strategies tried are unsuccessful.

Plan revision of subject work well before exam dates - encourage making notes, underlining key words, drawing tables/ pictures, etc. - when studying to aid memory.

6. Using Technology
Use of a computer to present homework often makes a positive difference to results in secondary school – both in subject work and in presentation of written work. Some schools now post homework tasks on the school website – so it is important to be able to access this. Remember that local libraries provide free Wi-Fi if things go wrong at home.

Access to audio/digital versions of subject textbooks, novels, etc. can greatly ease literacy requirements and ability to complete home and school work.